My thoguhts

Magdalena Palantzoglou

Presentation by *BookLeaf Publishing*

Web: www.bookleafpub.com

E-mail: info@bookleafpub.com

ISBN: 9789358315349

First edition 2023

To mum and dad,

Wherever you are

Thanks

For bringing me up

PREFACE

Hello,
This is my brain at its most raw form. A little getaway into the mind and thoughts of a bilingual girl finding her feet, and staying grounded.

Flat hunting 1/11

I have to chose a flat
I need to chose a flat
I would like to chose a flat
But why?
Why can't I stay where I am?
Why can't we take our next step?
We're not ready yet
I am not ready yet
I want my home
A home to enjoy

Things I would've said if I didn't have frontal lobe 2/11

This is a shit show
You can't fire her
The school will break down.
I've got a promotion
I didn't ask for it
I didn't apply for it
I got it.
No-one asked your opinion
It's a job
Suck it up and work
Do the singing.
What the fuck I'm doing here
You knew we were working till 4:30
Thanks for nothing, Cruella
What's the point of this?
Will I miss the 6:30?
Stop looking at me
Do I have monkeys in my head?
I've watched it, it's great
You don't smell good
No need to rush love, we are all getting off

Phew, finally no more lobe bra
Finally at home to say what I want

And what I want to say is
....

3/11

One glass of wine
Two glasses of wine
And then I'm done
One burger
Two burgers
How could I have fries
One episode
Two episodes
And I dozed off
One cuddle
Two cuddles
He tucks me in
I'm safe and sound

Perfect 4/11

Perfect morning,
Sex, shower, pancakes.
Not so good lunch time,
Coil, pain, expensive soup.
Better afternoon,
Tea, blanket, pride and prejudice.
Even better evening,
Wine, stew, tea.
Less better night,
Drugs, pain, sleepless.
A day, just like any.
Ups and downs
And downs and ups.
All together to bring
something resembling
a day in someone's life.

5/11

To feel good
Always taken for granted
Usually under-appreciated
Sometimes desired
Never
Today I don't feel good
First, my cramps
Then, my nose
Will I ever feel ok again?
I hope so. I know so. I want so.
Unless I can sleep as much as I want.
If so, then no. I rather feel poorly.

The wait 6/11

The wait for the drugs to kick in
For the train to come
For the bus to depart
For the kids to arrive
For the lunch time
The wait for the time to pass
For the report to be written
For the meeting to be finished
For the teachers to leave
For some quiet time
For the parent to stop talking
For the bus to turn up
For the next bus
The 2hs wait until my slot
To choose my dinner
For my dinner to be ready
To walk up the road
To wait two more minutes
To see the house
To meet everyone
To like everyone
For everyone to like me back
To leave the place
To walk to the station
To get the train

To change trains
To send the text
The real wait only begins now

7/11

If I could
I wouldn't work
But I'd get bored eventually
If I could
I'd live off the land
But would get tired eventually
If I could
I would read all day
But Id get distracted with the wind
If I could
Id cook all day
But id get grumpy and dirty and fat
If I could
Id write a book
But I don't even know where to start
If I could...
Id need too many lives to try all the ifs to this
life

8/11

My imaginary death
Would be somewhere safe
Neither here nor there
In a place in between.
Everyone would come together
To remember my worst bits
Some would talk about the good
But they rather get the drinks
Filthy martinis and Bloody's galore
Let's give them a good old dance
ABBA will come down
To carry me above
I'll be greeted at the gate
By my mum and by my dad
They will hug me in a sandwich
And show me the movie of my life
Best actor in leading role, of course,
would go to me
Having as my supporting actress
The bestest sister of them all
I bow in gratitude
And as the curtain draws
I get a microphone
And start
"The winner takes it all….."
ACTION

9/11

I've got nothing else to say
I'm tired
This is draining
Will you fucking do something without being
asked?
I can't anymore
I want to go
I'm tired of this
Maybe is my problem
Maybe I've made you an imbecile
Maybe it is me
I'm tired
I don't want to fight
Maybe I do want to fight
But what's the point
I've got nothing else to say

Breath 10/11

Today I had to remember to breath
Not only to stay alive
But not to choke
Breath to get air
And continue with the job
I had to breath
Even when I rather not
I had to breath even when the chest was close
breathing was good
To allow new life in
I took a deep breath and let it all go
Let go the week
Let go the bad
Let go the sad
Let it go out
Breath in again and start from scratch

Date 11/11

Wake up rested
Enjoying my time in bed
I always feel to tired
Specially after the last few days
Breakfast goes smoothly
I jump for a rinse
I chose my Clothes
And decide to shine
I have to get changed
Still going my style
This are the little things
That make me smile
The cool breeze
Brings new life
Enjoying the golf, the coffee, the walk
A good day in the bag
A day with hope
A day of resting
And planning for growth

Rest 12/11

Quiet calm day
Feeling content
Warm clothes on
No make up on
Relaxing at home
Nowhere to go
Just the two of us
Enjoying the both of us
Not rushing or sharing or showing
Just us at home
Relaxing alone

13/11

Today was a good day
A really good one
The sun shone out
The school was fun
I liked my clothes
And even worked out

14/11

What a beautiful thing it is
To have a friend in your life
Sometimes there more than one
And that's as much as you can ask
My friends are
Brilliant, loyal and supportive
With them I am invincible
Without them invisible
A life without friends would be
A quieter and grey one
I wish everyone would have
Friendships as strong as mine
Come rain or shine they are
Even if it's miles apart

15/11

Another good day
I'm starting to be suspicious
Suspicious of what?
It's been a few hard weeks
We're finally getting there
Contract signed
Move in date decided
All falling into place
I'm happy I've gone through this
I'm happy we've gone through this
We grew stronger and closer
It will be good to be alone
It will be good to miss us
I may miss this

16/11

Time alone
while being together
Haven't had much of it
And been craving a bit
I love being with you
I love being with me
I enjoy my own company
And look forward to
Finding my feet again
Enjoying our time apart
As much as our time together
And learning to be ourselves
Whilst learning to be a couple

17/11

I feel happy
It has been a fully happy week
I feel blessed to have people to see through me
That love me in my highs
And support me in my lows
People that care if I'm ok or not
I'm very grateful to have them with me
I'm very grateful to be back on my feet

18/11

Christmas is here and I love every bit
The atmosphere
The joy
The laughter
The familiarity
It makes people happy
Though it can make some quite sad
For me, tho the losses
It's a time to look back
Looking into what we were
What we are
What we'll be
And have a sweet little spot
For all that can be
I love this time of year
Time to reflect and set goals
They may be the same as last year
Or change for more growth

19/11

The days go by
Time passes
Slowly and fast
at the same time
I'm glad to be alive
As the days go by

20/11

Felt very much like a teacher
Spoke like a teacher
Dressed like a teacher
Walked like a teacher
What does that even mean?
I like being a teacher
I enjoy my job
Maybe I'd be good at a light admin role
But loose the class
Never at all
Maybe I'd be good at talking to parents
Convince them if things and get them to agree
But i prefer moulding minds of the future
That's way more rewarding
That's right for me

21/11

I love Theatre and what it entails
Different opportunities
Different points of view
Letting go of yourself
Enjoying the show
Not having to think about it
Just immersing in it all
Exploring what could be
In this fantasy we're told
Theatre is great
We see people express themselves
In a completely new light
Under the roles they play
Where they can be anybody else
Because that's it's beauty
It's a fantasy we're told

www.ingramcontent.com/pod-product-compliance
Lightning Source LLC
LaVergne TN
LVHW050251200726